LEVEL 1 SCIENCE

LET'S READ AND FIND OUT

SOUNDS ALL AROUND

BY WENDY PFEFFER · ILLUSTRATED BY ANNA CHERNYSHOVA

HARPER

An Imprint of HarperCollinsPublishers

With special thanks to Dr. John Milton Sooy at Rowan University and Dr. Agnieszka Roginska at New York University Steinhardt for their expert advice.

The Let's-Read-and-Find-Out Science book series was originated by Dr. Franklyn M. Branley, Astronomer Emeritus and former Chairman of the American Museum of Natural History–Hayden Planetarium, and was formerly co-edited by him and Dr. Roma Gans, Professor Emeritus of Childhood Education, Teachers College, Columbia University. Text and illustrations for each of the books in the series are checked for accuracy by an expert in the relevant field. For more information about Let's-Read-and-Find-Out Science books, write to HarperCollins Children's Books, 195 Broadway, New York, NY 10007, or visit our website at www.letsreadandfindout.com.

Let's Read-and-Find-Out Science® is a trademark of HarperCollins Publishers.

Sounds All Around

ISBN 978-0-06-238670-0 (trade bdg.) — ISBN 978-0-06-238669-4 (pbk.)

The artist used a Wacom pen, a tablet, and Adobe Photoshop to create the digital illustrations for this book.
Typography by Erica De Chavez
16 17 18 19 20 SCP 10 9 8 7 6 5 4 3 2 1 ❖ Newly Illustrated Edition, 2016

*For Sally, Milt, and Ad, who filled
my childhood with happy sounds*
—W.P.

*For Sonya, who fills my everyday life
with a bit too much sound sometimes*
—A.C.

Snap your fingers. Clap your hands. Whistle!
Clatter some pans! You're making sounds!

Crinkle-crunch through dry leaves.

Splish-splash in a puddle.

Make happy sounds!

Sad sounds!

Scary sounds!

Mad sounds!

Shake a can
of marbles . . .

Shake a can of
cheese puffs . . .

Shake a can
of pencils . . .

rattle, rattle, rattle.

pluff, pluff, pluff.

clank, clank, clank.

10

Your sounds fill the air.

Make more sounds.

Woof. Sing. Talk. Hum.

These sounds come out of your mouth, but they start in your throat.

11

Your Vocal Cords

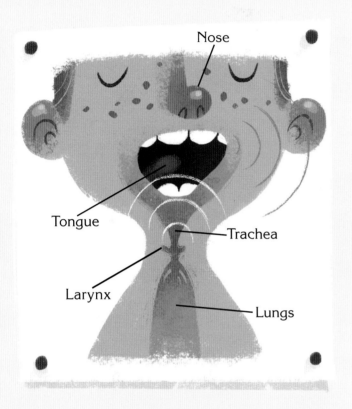

Nose

Tongue

Larynx

Trachea

Lungs

When you breathe out, air passes from your lungs through your larynx, which vibrates. The vibrations then travel through several air pockets, which change the way they sound—all to create your voice!

Feel your throat as you sing, talk, or hum. Your fingertips tingle because your **vocal cords** shake to make sounds.

They shake back and forth very fast. This is called vibrating. And that makes the air around them vibrate. These **vibrations** move through the air in waves called **sound waves**.

Now be quiet. Feel your throat. Your vocal cords are still.
They're not vibrating, so there's no sound.

A Look Inside an Ear

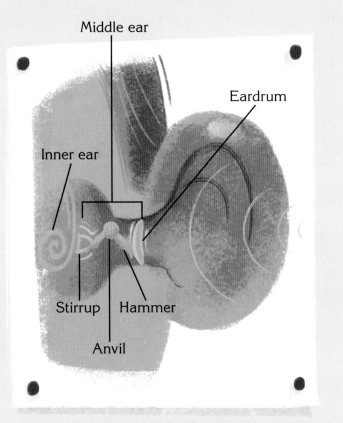

Middle ear

Eardrum

Inner ear

Stirrup | Hammer

Anvil

1. Sound moves through the ear and strikes the eardrum.
2. Sound waves cause the eardrum to vibrate, sending the bones in the middle ear into motion.
3. You hear sound.

You can't see sound waves, but when they reach your ear, tiny bones in your ear vibrate. Then you hear the sound.

Beating a drum makes it vibrate, and then the air around it vibrates. These vibrations ripple through the air. They travel from the drum to your ears, and you hear the sound of the drum.

Long ago, people used drum sounds to send messages. They beat high sounds, low sounds, fast sounds, and slow sounds.

These sounds traveled through the air from village to village. Different drumbeats sent different messages, such as "Rain clouds are forming" or "A new leader has been chosen."

People still use sounds to send messages. Clapping hands say, "Good job."

Clap

Knock, knock

A knock on the door asks, "Is anyone home?"

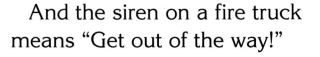

EEEEEEEE!

And the siren on a fire truck means "Get out of the way!"

18

Cluck, cluck, cluck

Animals use sounds to send messages, too.
A hen clucks to call her chicks.

Thump

A ruffed grouse makes
a drumming sound to
attract a mate.

HOWWWWL!

And a howler monkey roars to keep other
howlers out of its territory. A howler's roar
is one of the loudest animal sounds in the
world. No wonder other howlers stay away.

19

In the dark, a bat avoids an object in its flight path by making high squeaking sounds. Its sound waves hit the barn. The sound bounces back. These **echoes** warn the bat to change direction before it bumps into the barn.

A bat finds food using echoes, too. Sound waves bounce off insects. In total darkness, a bat can locate six hundred insects an hour by listening for the echoes. This is called **echolocation.**

Sound waves travel through solid ground as well as air. A snake has no ears. To hear, it puts its head on the ground. A bone in its head feels the sound vibrations. They warn the snake that an enemy, maybe a mongoose, lurks nearby.

Sound waves travel through water, too.
A mother whale can find her baby by
sending clicking sounds through the water.

When the sound waves bump into her calf, echoes bounce back. The mother whale listens. She hears the echoes and knows where her baby is.

Whales and dolphins locate objects by sending sounds through the water, then listening for echoes.

People use a device called **sonar** to send sounds in water. When the echoes bounce back, people know how deep the water is. They also discover where submarines, shipwrecks, and schools of fish are.

27

Sounds are an important part of our lives.

Some sounds, like music, please us.

Some sounds, like a jackhammer, annoy us.

Some sounds are quiet.

Some are loud.

How can you measure sounds?

How much you weigh
is measured in pounds.

How tall you stand is
measured in inches.

How loud you yell is measured in **decibels.**

Pssst . . . .

Whisper.
Whispering measures only about 30 decibels.

Hi.

Talk.
Talking measures about 60 decibels.

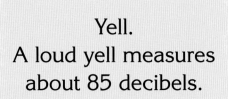

Wow!

Yell.
A loud yell measures about 85 decibels.

Rustling leaves measure only 20 decibels.
A vacuum cleaner 70 decibels.
Loud music 100 decibels.
A jackhammer 130 decibels.
A jet engine 140 decibels.

A space rocket is very loud. It measures 200 or more decibels.

31

Some loud sounds can really damage your ears, so you should be careful about protecting your ears around loud noises. Luckily, there are many ways to protect your ears, like covering your ears when a fire truck or ambulance drives by, or making sure you don't play music too loudly. People who are close to airplanes or use jackhammers have to be even more careful about protecting their hearing.

We live in a world of sounds. Telephones ring. Thunder rumbles. Water gurgles. Birds chirp. Bees buzz. Friends talk. And we laugh, cry, hiccup, and sigh.

Sounds are all around. Keep listening!

Glossary

Decibel—the unit for measuring how loud a sound is

Echo—a sound caused by sound waves bouncing back from a surface to the listener

Echolocation—a way of using echoes to find where objects are located, used by animals such as dolphins and bats

Sonar—a way of using echolocation to find where objects are located on the water or underwater

Sound wave—a special kind of invisible wave that is created when something is vibrating

Vibration—when something moves back and forth very quickly

Vocal cords—the parts of our throat that vibrate when air passes over them, allowing us to make sounds when we talk and sing

Sounds Matching Game

Setup:

1. Collect ten identical containers with lids—such as peanut cans.
2. With a Magic Marker put a red X on five cans. Put a blue X on the other five.
3. Put an equal amount of marbles into one red can and one blue can. Fill other pairs with paper clips, cotton, pennies, and rice.
4. Place the red cans together and the blue cans together.

Game Rules:

1. The first player shakes a red can, then a blue can. If both cans make the same sound, the player keeps the pair. If not, the cans must be returned.
2. Take turns. After a match is made, the player should guess what is in each can before opening it.
3. The player with the most pairs wins. Add other pairs to make the game more challenging.

Listen to Sounds around You

- Listen in the house. Do you hear a clock ticking, the television blaring, or someone laughing? What else do you hear?
- Listen on the front steps. Do you hear a dog barking, a ball bouncing, or a horn honking? What else do you hear?
- What could you hear on a farm? During a storm? In the forest? Near the ocean? By a brook? At the zoo? In the supermarket?

Listen to Sound Travel through Water

- In the bathtub keep your ears above the water. Ask an adult to knock on the side of the tub below the water level. Can you hear the knocking sound?
- Lie on your back with your ears under the water. Ask an adult to knock again. Can you hear the sound travel through water? Which knocking sounded louder?

This book meets the Common Core State Standards for Science and Technical Subjects. For Common Core resources for this title and others, please visit www.readcommoncore.com.

Be sure to look for all of these books in the Let's-Read-and-Find-Out Science series:

Level 1

The Human Body:
How Many Teeth?
I'm Growing!
My Feet
My Five Senses
My Hands
Sleep Is for Everyone
What's for Lunch?

Plants and Animals:
Animals in Winter
Baby Whales Drink Milk
Big Tracks, Little Tracks
Bugs Are Insects
Dinosaurs Big and Small
Ducks Don't Get Wet
Fireflies in the Night
From Caterpillar to Butterfly
From Seed to Pumpkin
From Tadpole to Frog
How Animal Babies Stay Safe
How a Seed Grows
A Nest Full of Eggs
Starfish
A Tree Is a Plant
What Lives in a Shell?
What's Alive?
What's It Like to Be a Fish?
Where Are the Night Animals?
Where Do Chicks Come From?

The World Around Us:
Air Is All Around You
The Big Dipper
Clouds
Is There Life in Outer Space?
Pop!
Snow Is Falling
Sounds All Around
The Sun and the Moon
What Makes a Shadow?

Level 2

The Human Body:
A Drop of Blood
Germs Make Me Sick!
Hear Your Heart
The Skeleton Inside You
What Happens to a Hamburger?
Why I Sneeze, Shiver, Hiccup, and Yawn
Your Skin and Mine

Plants and Animals:
Almost Gone
Ant Cities
Be a Friend to Trees
Chirping Crickets
Corn Is Maize
Dolphin Talk
Honey in a Hive
How Do Apples Grow?
How Do Birds Find Their Way?
Life in a Coral Reef
Look Out for Turtles!
Milk from Cow to Carton
An Octopus Is Amazing
Penguin Chick
Sharks Have Six Senses
Snakes Are Hunters
Spinning Spiders
Sponges Are Skeletons
What Color Is Camouflage?
Who Eats What?
Who Lives in an Alligator Hole?
Why Do Leaves Change Color?
Why Frogs Are Wet
Wiggling Worms at Work
Zipping, Zapping, Zooming Bats

Dinosaurs:
Did Dinosaurs Have Feathers?
Digging Up Dinosaurs
Dinosaur Bones
Dinosaur Tracks
Dinosaurs Are Different
Fossils Tell of Long Ago
My Visit to the Dinosaurs
What Happened to the Dinosaurs?
Where Did Dinosaurs Come From?

Space:
Floating in Space
The International Space Station
Mission to Mars
The Moon Seems to Change
The Planets in Our Solar System
The Sky Is Full of Stars
The Sun
What Makes Day and Night
What the Moon Is Like

Weather and the Seasons:
Down Comes the Rain
Feel the Wind
Flash, Crash, Rumble, and Roll
Hurricane Watch
Sunshine Makes the Seasons
Tornado Alert
What Will the Weather Be?

Our Earth:
Archaeologists Dig for Clues
Earthquakes
Flood Warning
Follow the Water from Brook to Ocean
How Deep Is the Ocean?
How Mountains Are Made
In the Rainforest
Let's Go Rock Collecting
Oil Spill!
Volcanoes
What Happens to Our Trash?
What's So Bad About Gasoline?
Where Do Polar Bears Live?
Why Are the Ice Caps Melting?
You're Aboard Spaceship Earth

The World Around Us:
Day Light, Night Light
Energy Makes Things Happen
Forces Make Things Move
Gravity Is a Mystery
How People Learned to Fly
Light Is All Around Us
Simple Machines
Switch On, Switch Off
What Is the World Made Of?
What Makes a Magnet?
Where Does the Garbage Go?